The Complete Liturgical Poetry

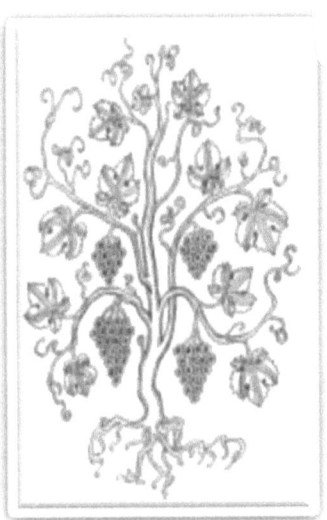

of

Adam of St. Victor

Volume 1

Revelation Insight Publishing Co.

2010

Dear Reader

1 Corinthians 2: 7-15. We speak the hidden mystical wisdom of God, which God ordained before the world unto our Glory, Which none of the princes of this world knew, for had they known it, they would not have crucified the Lord of Glory. But, as it is written, eye has not seen, nor ear heard, neither has it entered into the Heart of man to conceive the things, which God has prepared for them that Love him. However, God has revealed them unto us by His Spirit, for the Spirit searches all things, yes, and the deep things of God. For what man knows the things of a man, save the spirit of a man, which is in him? Even so, the thing of God knows no man, but the Spirit of God. Now we have received, not the Spirit of this world, but the Spirit, which is of God; that we might know the things that are freely given us of God. Which things also we speak, not in your words which man's wisdom teaches, but which the, Holy Spirit teaches, comparing spiritual things with Spiritual. However, the natural man receives not the things of the Spirit of God, for they are foolishness unto him, neither can he know them, because they are spiritually discerned. Nevertheless, he that is spiritual judges or discerns all things.

THE COMPLETE LITURGICAL POETRY

of

ADAM OF ST. VICTOR

Spiritual Poetry Series Vol. 1

Behold I stand at the door and knock, if anyone hears my voice and opens the door; I will come in and dine with him, and he with Me. He who overcomes, I will grant to sit down with Me on My throne, as I also overcame and with My Father on His throne. " Rev 3: 21

All rights reserved. No part of this book may be reproduced or transmitted in any form or means, electronic or mechanical including photocopying, or by any information storage and retrieval system without permission in writing from Revelation Insight.

ISBN # 978-1-936392-02-5

Library of Congress Cataloging in Publication Data.

#2010929280

BAISAC # REL012120

Printed and bound in the USA

Revelation – Insight © 2010

E Mail: Mystic@Orthodox.com

General Introduction

These are designed and presented to accent a fine library of the essentials required for further in depth investigation of this genre.

The focus of this series is to provide today's reader with the essentials of background and investigative writings that are a part of our Christian heritage. The selected written works are a culmination of screening the best of this genre from the numerous documents, which are available. We selected these works based on a number of factors. The greatest impact upon the body of Christ, their insight of the genre and their related impact on other writers and the feasibility of this text to be used as a guide, in a standalone application. They are the primary indicators used, coupled with other factors in making our selection.

Each text in this series is a premier stand-alone text in this genre. The intended corpus of works pooled together make for a reference library rivaling that of some great monastery or university library on this subject. These are re-edited for today's reader. These writings are not abridged, they are the complete text, completely redone in grammar, syntax, verbiage, and other literary components to ensure the spirit of these works are not lost in these important changes.

For many of these texts, this is the first time they are available in this format and to these standards. These are not a scholarly reference work edition. For that purpose, there are other publications available. This series is intended for those who have a fundamental familiarity with the subject, and some of the writers. The intent is to address the needs of the readers who are journeying forward on their quest in union with God. There are other selections to be added as certain texts are processed. Please look forward to these great works in print, audio and E-book formats at your local bookstore, although us directly.

Spiritual Poetry Series Forward

The staff at "Revelation-Insight" presents this series. The objective of this particular series is to provide the focused reader, student, and others who have a need to go beyond the fundamental basics and achieve something more. This series was designed to provide you with the necessary tools by Thomas Aquinas to have a ready answer to foundational subject matter and answers to key and essential portions of various philosophical and theological works.

These tools will come in the form of apologies, a historical reference, systematic theology and various dissertations. This particular work, which is more than an overview of the accumulative life's effort and its varied formularies; it is an insightful guide. Presenting you with the essential and fundamental key elements required in answering a bevy of questions and perhaps summarizing the information with a need for a deeper explanation.

Throughout this series, there will be additions, which could be considered not simply a reference work but much more, and indeed that is our aim. By, providing you with much more than you intended upon receiving and yet not to the point of becoming overwhelmed. This is our pledge to you the consumer, to always bring to you in a palatable formula and format. To the student, a ready reference, to the reader, to educate through pertinent information, to the educator an essential reference tool for all avenues and venues. This is what we inspire to become for you the consumer. Many times libraries have bits and pieces spread across numerous volumes, requiring numerous hours to comb through. This series is designed and produced to provide you with the correct and proper information you need to come to grasp and obtain a sure foundation in your understanding your history belief events, leading up to its current formulary. Since history is what it is, and the facts remain self evident, in this series, we will not subscribe nor slant our presentations, following particular denominations. We will present these as straightforward as numbers are in a math equation. The rational is the numbers and the equation is what it is. There is no need to interpret. There is only one way to solve, one way to proceed, and only one correct answer to grasp.

Editor's Notes

Rational, Method and Aim of This Modernization

The intention of this book is not for the scholar. Instead, it is for the pilgrim who does not have access, to such works. It is for such individuals, that this edition has been prepared. My aim has been to make Adam of St Victor's meaning clear to the modern reader with as little alteration of the available texts as possible. I have modernized the spelling, have simplified long and involved constructions, and have tried to illuminate the meaning by careful punctuation. I have dealt sparingly with the vocabulary, striving to keep some of the words likely to be understood.

I am aware that by my modernization, I have laid myself open to criticism in many directions. I strove for consistency, and tried solely to retain as far as possible the simplicity and charm of the original spirit and intent

I have dismissed most of the Latin verbiage and some notes.

I have retained the "King's English" in the rhyme.

<u>This text is presented in its entirety. It remains unabridged.</u>

FROM THE TEXT OF GAUTIER,

WITH TRANSLATIONS INTO ENGLISH IN THE

DIGBY S. WRANGHAM, M.A.,

ST. John's College, oxford,

Vicar of Darrington, Yorkshire.

Original Preface

In offering this work to the public I am breaking what is practically new ground to the great majority of English readers. The circumstances, detailed in the introduction to M. Gautier's Edition, of which the larger part of the poetry of Adam of St. Victor was entirely lost to the world for many years after the French Revolution. In this day and age, it appears to be a great to give an interest and novelty regarding it in this country at this day from the only other English Edition, published in Paris in 1858- 9, has only to a very limited degree been averted. I feel therefore that, so far as the original text is concerned, I am doing a good service to the lovers of Medieval Hymnology, by rendering it more accessible to them in this, by using the first edition of it, published in England, and reviving it before it enters into obscurity.

Now regarding what forms the principal part of my work in these volumes, viz., the translations, I feel, on the other hand, that a great apology is due for the imperfections with which I know they abound, and I am anxious therefore to explain the principles, which have guided me in my attempts for they are no better than attempts to render the original into our language.

I have looked at the duty of a translator as equivalent to that of an engraver, and felt that, the poet being a "word painter" the translator must be a "word engraver;" in other words that to be successful, he must reproduce faithfully, as a whole and in detail, what he sets himself to copy. A so called translation, which is stripped at the taste of the translator not only of the form of the original, viz., its meter, but more or less also of the thoughts and expressions with which that form is clothed, appears to me to fail to be what it professes to be, just in proportion as these defects, if I may venture to call them so, appear in it. It may be a very beautiful piece of poetry in itself, and it very often is so, but a translation, i.e., a transferring of a given original from one language into another it can scarcely be.

If I were to take the picture of a beautiful boy with curling locks and "fair and of a muddy countenance," and draw another, as fancy led me, of that same boy in later life, bronzed in the battle of life, of an athletic form and with a flowing beard, although I might keep the pleasing features of the original face before me constantly and reproduce their outline carefully, no one could say that I had made a copy of the picture I had seen.

Those who saw the two portraits together might detect that the child was the father of the man, but that would be all. They would count the two as separate works of are, standing or falling by their own several faults or merits, and never dream that the second was intended to reproduce the first.

What is true of the copyist would seem to be necessarily still truer of the engraver, who has not the help of colors to aid his efforts, as the former has, and is compelled therefore to follow most closely his original both in outline and detail, if he would have that original recognizable at all in the somber hues of his engraving.

In like manner the translator, so far from needing the originality with which some would have him endowed, must be content, I submit, like the engraver, to follow his original painfully, line after line, and not be satisfied with his work till he has succeeded in so reconstructing it, as to leave no doubt upon the mind of the reader of the two works as to their inter identity. In a certain sense, no doubt, an engraver should be an artist, that is to say, he should have a good eye for proportion, and be well versed in the rules of drawing generally; and in the same sense a translator should be something of a poet, with a good ear for rhythm, of proportion of poetry, and not ignorant of the rules of poetical composition. Yet neither engraver nor translator needs to be original, to my mind; for, when his originality comes in at the window, his original goes out at the door. It is a singular fact, for I think it is a fact, that great poets have not been very successful translators, nor successful translators, very great poets. Exceptions there may have been to this rule, but very rare ones. The only great poet who was I can scarcely say a great, but a good translator, that I can call to mind, was Dryden, and his translations are of the freest; while the merits of Milton, Pope, Cowper, Shelley and Keble, as translators, pale before those of Gilford, Neale, Fi'ere and Conington.

Should I seem to go too far were I to suggest that the object of a translator and that of a parodist should be much the same in kind, however different in effect? The difference between them appears to me to be simply this, viz., that, while both preserve the meter of their original, the translator changes its language, and preserves, as far as possible, its meaning, and the parodist changes its meaning, and, as far as possible, preserves its language.

If in these principles, which I cannot help thinking should govern translators, I am at all right, however imperfect may be, and are, my own attempts to carry them out, I need scarcely point out how absolutely essential it is to observe them in translating such an author as Adam of St. Victor, because it is "manner" and not "matter" that is his distinguishing characteristic. Adam's range is not great;" and, therefore, if you take away his meters, which are ever changing even in the same sequence, and his peculiar mode of building them up, until he finishes with a rush of liquid rhyme, you utterly efface what is his distinguishing feature. No author probably is so difficult to translate such at least was Dr. Neale's opinion, and he had had experience enough of the difficulty to make him a judge; but, if translated at all, it can only be fairly done by adhering strictly to the lines upon which Adam himself builds his mellifluous superstructure. It is better, to my delight, to present even the skeleton of him, as one may hope to succeed in doing, in a perfectly literal translation; than to give him to the world as a shapeless mummy, embalmed though it may be in the richest pieces of original thought and feeling.

At the same time I would not be understood to maintain that no license at all is permitted to the translator; own versions of Adam of St. Victor would be more faulty, than I quite feel they are as it is, were that the case. I simply urge that the license must at any rate be limited, in the case of additions or omissions, to such as leave intact the sense of the original passages, and, in the case of meters, to, at most, the occasional varying the rhythm of some of them, leaving the number of syllables the same. Such a meter as the following, e.g., and there are some four or five of that character in Adam's collection of sequences, appears to me to be one, that it is almost impossible in our consonant ridden language to reproduce faithfully and yet gracefully.

>   Salve, dies dierum Gloria.
>
>   Dies felLx, Christi Victoria.
>
>   Dies digna jugi lastitia.
>
>   Dies prima!

I have ventured, therefore, to alter the emphasis, while keeping intact the length, of each line in this example;

>   Hail, day, the glory of all days! to thee!
>
>   Thrice happy day, Christ's day of victory!
>
>   The first day, day most fit continually
>
>   Our joy to show!

I have adopted the same course, and for the same reason, in the case of four other Sequences, viz.: "Gaude Sion, qu»diem recolis;" "Jerusalem et Sion filise;" "Aquas plenasamaritudine;" and "Gratiani gi ata solempnitas." A few lines, sprinkled about here and there in other Sequences, I have treated in the same way. With these exceptions, I have kept, I believe, rigidly to the exact meter of each original Sequence.

One great difficulty in carrying out the principle of literal translation in these volumes has been not only the number, but the character also, of the rhymes so called for. English rhymes are naturally, and generally, single rhymes; Latin rhymes, on the other hand, are naturally, and generally, double rhymes. In Latin, again, the same terminations, if attached to words of different meanings, are held to rhyme; in English, however, this is not the case, every word, in order to make a good rhyme, must in our language have a different termination, ultimate or penultimate, according as the rhyme is single or double, to the word with which it is meant to rhyme.

The literal translator, therefore, of any aspiring Latin poetry, especially one that ventures, in translating such a master of rhyme as Adam of St. Victor, to keep intact both the number and the character of the original rhymes, starts, handicapped, as it were, by the necessity of finding rhymes in numbers far greater than any English poetry, so far as I know, contains, and of a kind in which the English language is singularly poor. I venture to remind the critical reader of these facts, in the hope that they may serve to explain, if not to excuse, my shortcomings, which I am painfully aware of in the matter of rhymes. I can only say that I have done my best to avoid even doubtful rhymes, and such as still disfigure my translations remain, because I have failed to find better ones to replace them.

I have thought it better on the whole, chiefly in the interest of the translations, not to print the original sequences and my own renderings of them upon opposite pages. I am aware that some, who will value the book simply for the sake of the Latin text, would have preferred having the translations printed at the end of each volume by themselves, but the poetry of Adam of St. Victor is of so peculiar a kind, that I think the majority of any readers I may be fortunate enough to secure, will like better to not have the two placed as they arc for the sake of ready comparison. The translations, if found to be tolerably correct, are naturally such an interpretation of the originals as to render long critical notes unnecessary, and such as there are I have remitted to the end of each volume, so as not to interfere with the appearance of the pages.

The notes themselves are principally confined to short accounts of the less known Saints commemorated by the poet, to Scripture references, and to explanations of the typology and symbolism of both of which Adam is very fond contained in the Sequences. I have gathered my information from the best, indeed the only, sources accessible to me in a country parsonage. I should like to be able to thank by name all those who have aided me in many ways in my undertaking, but they are so many in number that I am compelled to content myself with a general expression of heartfelt gratitude in the case of the large majority of my kindly coadjutors. Some, however, I feel bound to mention more particularly.

A Historical Perspective of the "Victorines"

WHO ARE THE VICTORINES

ADAM of ST. VICTOR:

The Abbey of St. Victor, from which the great Latin hymnologist takes his name, and which, originally, was in the suburbs of Paris, was later on absorbed into the city itself, as she enlarged her borders, was celebrated, especially in the twelfth century, as a school of theology.

Probably no other religious foundation could boast of such a brilliant triad of doctors of divinity, as the one that graced this Abbey during that century in the persons of Hugh of St. Victor, known to his generation as the "Second Augustine;" his pupil, Richard of St. Victor, named Alter Augustine; and Adam of St. Victor, the author of the Sequences in these volumes, who, as will be apparent to the most cursory reader was even deeply versed in the learning of the school to which he belonged. If you were to place a "Greek" perspective, Hugh could be considered as Socrates, followed by his pupil Plato (Richard) and subsequently, Aristotle, (Andrew). The rational that I assert here is quite simple really; Hugh and Richard both followed an allegorical analysis of the scriptures, where as Andrew, like Chrysostom and Jerome, took a more straight forward approach. In the early days of the Christian church, there were two fundamental schools of thought: those who were form the "Antioch" side, and those of the "Alexandrian" segment. The Antioch's were literal, while the Alexandrian's were metaphorical. Thus, down through the ages and on into today's church, there remain these two formulary schools.

Beyond the fact, however, that they were monks of St. Victor, whose residence there one or other of them covered nearly the whole of the twelfth century, the accounts that we have left of them are exceedingly meager and uncertain; these being Andrew, a disciple under Richard and Archard. Andrew is considered as the "Second Jerome." Walter was also an abbot, but was an anti-intellectual, he wrote against Peter Abelard. They live for us now in days, very much as they must have lived, in the retirement of their monastic life, for their contemporaries, only in the books which they "Sequence." The prolongation of the versicle of the Alleluia, instituted in order to give the deacon time to reach the pulpit to chant the Gospel. Gradually words were set to this cadence, and so came the Sequence. It is ascribed alike to St. Notker and Alcuin; the Sequences in rhythm are a development of later days.

Originally the Sequence was called a Prose, because its early' form was rhythmical prose. Orby Shipley's "Glossary of Ecclesiastical Terms" (1872), wrote, of which, in all probability, we know more than their own generation did. Hugh of St. Victor, the oldest of them, was by birth a Saxon; when he entered the Monastery of St. Victor we are not told. All we can glean about his chronology is that he died there either in A.D. 1139, or one of the two following years.

Richard of St. Victor, his pupil, and a native of Scotland, was more closely contemporaneous with Adam, the last and most brilliant of the three. There seems no reason to doubt that he was nearly of the same age as the latter, though his life was by no means so prolonged as that of Adam, if we are to accept the authority of an old MS., quoted by Gautier, as quoted by John of Toulouse; which describes the poet as being *"Richard Victoriana contemporaneous, sed longe superstes."*

Regarding Adam of St. Victor so scanty are the materials for a biographical notice of him), we cannot certainly prove even the nationality. This much only seems to be certain, that he was a native either of England or Brittany. He is described generally in the MSS. of the period immediately succeeding his own as Brito, and the question remains, and must remain, unsettled, as to which of the two countries for which he is claimed as a native, that term refers. Of course in an Abbey where so many of the monks were evidently foreigners, for neither Hugh nor Richard were Frenchmen, it is possible that the great Medieval poet was a fellow countryman of ours; but Archbishop Trench and it is a point upon which, as upon most others, we may safely defer to his better judgment concludes, that "the fact that France was the main seat of Latin poetry in the twelfth century, and that all the most famous composers in this kind, as Hildebert, the two Bernards, Abelard, Marbod, Peter the Venerable, were Frenchmen, leaves it more likely that he, the first and fore most of all, was such as well!"

M. Gautier entertains no doubt, and he has evidently been most indefatigable in his researches into all that relates personally, or poetically, to the object of them, that, be he "Breton" or "Briton," Adam entered the religious foundation of St. Victor, as a young man, about A.D. 1130; after having, as Archbishop Trench says, "made his studies at Paris." Here he remained for the rest of his life, which was prolonged certainly to A.D. 11 72, and probably, according to M. Gautier, to A.D. 1192. And here he wrote at various times, as the occasion called each forth, the series, and it is not a short one, of the sequences on which his claim to literary honors mainly rests, and of which a great deal of English Churchmen must, in many points, decline to follow their doctrinal teaching very few will fail to recognize the exceeding beauty, looked at as classical compositions merely, and fewer still, one would hope, to appreciate at their real value the exactness of their author's theology when dealing with the great Catholic doctrines which are common to almost the whole of Christendom, or the devotional spirit that breathes throughout his writings.

Lord Coleridge, the present Lord Chief Justice of England, in his preface to a republication by him in 1872 of the seventeenth century edition in English of "A Mirror of Monks," by Lewis Blosius, (which we will produce later) expresses so completely the sentiments by which I have been animated in dealing with the works of Adam of St. Victor, that I gladly and gratefully avail myself of his lordship's permission to quote a few sentences from it here, feeling sure that the reader will be glad to have an opinion on such a point from one whose opinion upon any point must carry great weight with it

"It is hardly necessary to say that I do not agree with every theological doctrine which Blosius assumes or inculcates in his book; but I think the book in itself a good and beautiful book. I believe the writer of it to have been a holy man; and I do not think it right, in spite of high authority to the contrary, to mutilate or adapt such works as these. To do so appears to me unmanly and unfair. It is as if we were afraid of the soundness of our convictions, and dared not look in the face the fact that good men of other times did not share them. Whereas it is part of Christian history that very good and saintly men have held opinions in religion which we now think mistaken; and it is a narrow and shallow judgment which holds such opinions to be inconsistent with true and vital Christianity. This book, to my mind, proves that they are nowise inconsistent: and I most earnestly hope that those who read it carefully will think so too."

The reader will have the opportunity of judging for themselves as to the merits of the various sequences as they come before him; but it may be well, perhaps, to say a few words as to their general character, and I know not that they can be said better than by one who has so thoroughly identified his name with Latin hymnology generally, and especially with that of the "Victorine School," as the present Archbishop (Trench) of Dublin:

"Very different estimates have been formed of the merits of Adam of St. Victor's hymns. His most zealous admirers will hardly deny that he pushes too far, and plays overmuch with, his skill in the typical application of the Old Testament. So, too, they must own that sometimes he is unable to fuse his manifold learned allusion into the passion of his poetry. . . . Nor less must it be allowed that he is sometimes guilty of conceits, of plays upon words, not altogether worthy of the solemnity of his theme.

Thus of one Martyr he says,

' Sub securi stat securus; '

of another. Saint [Vincent] namely: —

' Dum torretur, non terretur;

of the Blessed Virgin (for he did not escape, as it was not to be expected that he should, the exaggerations of his time),

' O dulcis vena venise; '

of heaven: —

' O quam beata curia,

Qus curse prorsus nescla.'

Sometimes, too, he is over fond of displaying feats of skill in versification, or prodigally accumulating, or curiously interlacing his rhymes, that he may show his perfect mastery of the forms which he is using, and how little he is confined or trammeled by them.

"These faults it will be seen, yet most are indeed of them but merits pushed into excess. Even accepting them as defects, his profound acquaintance with the whole circle of the theology of his time, and eminently with its exposition of Scripture; the abundant and admirable use, with indeed the drawback already mentioned, which he makes of it. Delivering as he does with his poems from the merely subjective cast of those, beautiful as they are, of St. Bernard, the exquisite are and variety with which for the most part his verse is managed and his rhymes disposed, their rich melody multiplying and ever deepening at the close. The strength which he often concentrates into a single line, his skill in conducting a story, and, most of all, the evident nearness of the things, which he celebrates to his own heart of hearts. All these, and other excellencies, render him, as far as my judgment goes, the foremost among the sacred Latin poets of the Middle Ages." (Tim, use for back cover)

"He may have no single poem to vie with the austere grandeur of the Dies Irœ, nor yet with the tearful passion of the Stabat Mater, although concerning the last point there might well be a question; but then it must not be forgotten that these stand well nigh alone in the names of ' Thus of a Roman governor, who, alternating flatteries with threats, is seeking to bribe St. Agnes from her allegiance to Christ by the offer of worldly dignities and honors,"

"Offert multa, spondet plura,

Periturus peritura."

Their respective authors, while from his ample treasure house I shall enrich this volume with a multitude of hymns, all of them of considerable, some of the very highest, merit. Indeed, were I disposed to name any one who might dispute the palm of sacred Latin poetry with him, it would not be one of these, but rather Hildebert, Archbishop of Tours."

It would be unnecessary for me, even if I were able, which I am not, to add much to this eloquent and exhaustive summary of the merits, and defects as well, of this great poet. One point only, in what is characteristic of the author, is not touched upon, and that is his love of alliteration, carried at times perhaps to an excess like his play upon words,' but often used with striking effect.

The history of the Sequences in this work is a curious and a checkered one. As I said at the beginning of this notice, the Abbey of St. Victor, which in our poet's time was in the suburbs of Paris, was by the growth of the town afterwards included within its walls. There it remained undisturbed, and having Adam of St. Victor's poetry in its library, until the French Revolution, when, in common with all others, its religious foundation was dissolved, its inmates dispersed, and its precious MSS. removed, as it appeared afterwards, to the National Library in the Louvre. Some of Adam's Sequences had, during the centuries that the MSS. remained in the custody of the monks of the author's monastery, found their way into circulation, thirty-seven of them with his name attached to them, and a few others without any trace of them.

Take this instance from the Sequence, "On the Passion of St. Quintin,"

" Propter jugum Christi lene,

Premunt compes et catense

Carcerali clausum cella;

Sed triumphat bonus bene

Universum genus poense,

Famem, frigus, et flagella."

The thirty seven were collected and published by Ciichtoveus, a Roman Catholic theologian of the first half of the sixteenth century, in his "Elucidatorium Ecclesiasticum," which passed through several editions from 1515 to 1556 at Paris, Basle, and Geneva. This work, which was written originally for the instruction of the clergy in the meaning of the various offices of the Church, according to Archbishop Trench, became invaluable to those who made Mediaeval Hymnology their study, and was in fact the only collection of it on a large scale.

The remainder of the Sequences contained in these volumes, and which never saw the light (until they were discovered in the Louvre) from the date of the French Revolution up to the middle of this century, we owe to the persevering search after them which M. Gautier made about the latter date. Those published by him for the first time are forty-eight in number, and include some of the most striking of the whole collection. Of three the first line only survives, the remainder of the Sequences not having been found as yet; and it is more than probable that there may be more still written by Adam, which cannot be assigned to him now, because it is a remark able fact that, numerous as those hymns are of which he will henceforth have the credit, we do not possess a single Sequence of which he was professedly the author, upon so central a Christian truth as the Passion of our Lord, or one for Lent or Advent, which could hardly, one would imagine, have been the case always, seeing that the rest of the Christian year is so largely illustrated in his writings.

The collection, as M. Gautier gave it to the world, consisted of 106 "Sequences", satisfactorily proved to have come from Adam of St. Victor's pen, viz., thirty seven published and attributed to the author by Ciichtoveus, two published by him without attribution, seventeen published in other collections without attribution, forty seven published for the first time by Gautier, and the three mentioned above of which we have as yet only the first line. Besides these, however, there is the Epitaph of Adam, of which only the first ten lines were written by him, and eight Sequences doubtfully or wrongly attributed to him, but included in M. Gautier's volumes.

All these, arranged as they were in the French edition, will be found in that now offered to the public. The reader will, no doubt, be struck by the great variety of meters employed by the poet, not only in the Sequences, taken as a whole, but also in single Sequences. In some the meters changes several times during the course of them, and even single stanzas are constantly subjected to the same process. The effect is to give great variety to the hymns, generally and singly, enabling the poet to introduce an amount of light and shade into his compositions, which is impossible when one meter is rigidly adhered to throughout a poem. As all Adam's Sequences were originally set to music and used in the worship of his Abbey, a suggestion is perhaps allowable on my part, as to whether we might not now a days have some of the music in our choral services arranged upon a similar plan. As it is, we have nothing between the ordinary hymn in which the meter never changes, and for which, therefore, the same tune must be used throughout, and anthems, which, beautiful as they are, are far too elaborate and difficult for general use in our churches.

The arrangement of these Mediaeval hymns appears to me to combine the advantages, without the defects, of both hymns and anthems, possessing as they do all the simplicity of the first without their sameness, and much of the variety of the last without their elaborateness. If we could vary the tunes in a single hymn, as is often done, as it is, in the Te Deum or the Psalms of the day, we should be enabled to increase not only the length of the hymns, which are now confined to four or six verses, but to add to their devotional effect as well by having both the meter in which, and the music to which the words are set somewhat more appropriate to the sentiments sought to be expressed than is always the case now.

CONTENTS OF THE FIRST VOLUME

SEQUENCES FOR CHURCH SEASONS

CONTENTS

Christmas

The Circumcision of Christ

Easter

Ascension

Pentecost

Trinity

On the Dedication of a Church

Sequences for Saints

Days

Notes

SEQUENCES FOR CHURCH SEASONS

HRISTMAS

The Creator, not by nature

But by might, becomes a creature,

That with glory the Creator

May His creature once more crown.

Presaged in the prophets' pages,

He, Who of no place or age is,

Enters on our life's brief stages.

Not relinquishing His own.

Virgin still, the creature gives

Birth to Him through Whom she lives;

Maiden's womb her spouse conceives;

Daughter's breasts her father feed.

Nature's law no instance knows

Of such birth as this one shows

And, since it all law o'erthrows,

Nature trembles at the deed.

Heaven to earth has condescended;

Man is with the Godhead blended,

And the Man God is attended

HRISTMAS

By celestial ministry.

That, as priest, is consecrated

Heaven's king, is demonstrated;

Peace on earth is promulgated,

Glory unto God on high!

You ask why? How? This beginneth.

Why? Because mankind first sinneth;

How? God's just will then combineth

With His grace to break sin's thrall.

O how sweet their blended savor,

Changing into spiced wine's flavor,

When Christ tasted, man to favor.

Bitter vinegar and gall!

O dread mystery, soul reviving!

When Samaria's son arriving

Sets, for wounds a balm contriving,

On His own beast those that fall!

He, Elisha's true successor,

God man, counted a transgressor.

To the Shunamite, to bless her,

Has restored her son again.

As a giant runs He joying,

Who, His shoulder's strength employing,

Bears His sheep. Death's law destroying,

Back to primal joys of men.

CHRISTMAS

As God man He lives and reigns,

And lost man from hell restrains;

Man with joy heaven's realms obtains,

Filling up its orders ten.

Heaven's Sire's mother, goal of sages!

Pray that Father through all ages,

Tell thy Son to point our stages

To where peace and glory reign;

Till there, being

Braced, God seeing,

Lift we Alleluia's strain,

Let creation say " Amen! "

HRISTMAS

In the highest, hark! the strain,

" Glory to the new born King!

Who doth with Him peace, again

Joining earth and heaven, bring! "

Honor thus is paid aright

Unto this, Christ's natal morn;

At Whose birth the grace so bright

Of a new made law is born.

The appointed Mediator,

Our salvation's price to pay, lo

Not His share in human nature,

But its misdeeds, puts away.

Not a whit less bright appearing,

The life giving star we see;

Nor does Mary by child bearing

Lose her spotless chastity.

HRISTMAS

What is this rock stone so precious,

Quarried not by hand, but Jesus,

Scion of a line of kings,

Who, begot, without man's aid,

Of a pure yet pregnant maid.

From her fleshly nature springs?

Let the desert blossom forth;

Joy, waste places of the earth!

Jesse's rod doth flowers unfold.

Root it branches, branch it bloometh,

Virgin born, a Savior cometh,

As the law of old foretold.

David's self that root portended;

Mary is that branch, descended

From that seed of royal line

He, the Son unto us given,

Is its flower, a flower from heaven.

Since its fragrance is divine.

He, Whose birth's due celebration

Forms the angels' proclamation,

In a manger cradle lies;

Heavenly hosts therein delight,

Whilst the shepherds watch by night

'Neath the silence of the skies.

CHRISTMAS

All things shouts of joy upraise

For the Virgin's Son most high;

Him the law and psalms too praise

With the page of prophecy.

Angels', shepherds', salutations,

Stars' and wise men's indications,

In their object all agree:

Haste those Eastern kings where, crying,

In a crib a Babe is lying,

Who the Gentile first fruits be.

Infant Jesus, death bound never!

For a time and yet for ever!

By Your might mankind deliver

From this life's adversity:

When this mortal life is ended,

From this living death ascended,

By Your clemency befriended,

Grant us deathless life with Thee!   Amen.

CHRISTMAS

Since a Savior is born for us,

With the angels in glad chorus

Let our race unite to day:

Sweetly sound such hymns uprising,

Different voices harmonizing

All their praises in one lay.

Happy day, when the Supernal,

With the Father co eternal,

Of a Virgin comes to birth!

Day of joy and jubilation,

When the bright illumination

Of the true Sun lights glad earth!

God has a Redeemer given,

His, the Father's, Son from heaven.

That the sinner should not die

It is grace alone, not merit.

Gives us new life through the Spirit,

Visiting God's family.

HRISTMAS

Infinite and in all places,

He, whom sense and earth's wide spaces

Comprehend not nor contain,

Though eternal, time obeys,

And, though everywhere, here stays,

All things to restore again!

He sin's form, without sin, wears,

And, to be made like us, shares

Our worn out existence here

That the temporal and eternal,

That the spiritual and carnal.

Natures might thus linked appear.

So the Word and Flesh and Spirit

Doth one Person thus inherit

In mysterious union,

That no change its nature shows.

Nor two fold that Person grows,

But is altogether one.

This great mystery lies ever

Hidden from man's base deceiver,

And at fault his malice is;

That the wisdom of the Godhead

'Neath the veil of flesh is shrouded

Our blind enemy ne'er sees.

HRISTMAS

This deep mystery's complication

No abstruse investigation

By induction can explain.

'Tis not mine to know its measure,

But I wot that God's good pleasure

Rules where reason cannot strain.

O how deep the counsel of God appears!

How sublime the mystery it declares!

Rod a flower,

Fleece a shower,

And a Son a Virgin bears.

Her conception hurt not her chastity,

Nor its blooming that ever verdant tree;

In conceiving

And birth giving,

Lily like, still pure is she!

Mary, star of ocean! giving

To this shipwrecked age we live in '

After God its hope alone!

See what rival machinations,

And what fierce and dire temptations

Vex us sorely every one.

Virtue unto us be given,

And demonic pride be driven

Far away from us by Thee;

HRISTMAS

To Your offspring O commend us,

Lest His brief but most tremendous

Sentence crush us utterly.

Jesus, Who is our salvation,

Who its wondrous operation

With such wisdom watches over!

Those, who keep this day, defending,

Here Your help to them extending,

Grant them joy for evermore!

HRISTMAS

For the Gentiles up has sprung

Light, for those that sate among

Darkness and in death's deep gloom.

Joys a people all forlorn,

That on earth a Child is born

From a spotless maiden's womb.

Guilty man to raise to heaven.

Condescends the God man even

To our nature's misery.

Who would not with joy be praising,

Songs of wondering gladness raising,

Grace work of such novelty?

What is more full of bliss,

What is more fathomless,

Than such a mystery?

How worthy all our praise,

How unlike human ways,

Is God's humility!

HRISTMAS

This deep mystery's complication

No abstruse investigation

By induction can explain.

'Tis not mine to know its measure,

But I wot that God's good pleasure

Rules where reason cannot strain.

O how deep the counsel of God appears!

How sublime the mystery it declares!

Rod a flower,

Fleece a shower,

And a Son a Virgin bears!

Her conception hurt not her chastity.

Nor its blooming that ever verdant tree;

In conceiving

And birth giving,

Lily like, still pure is she!

Mary, star of ocean! giving

To this shipwrecked age we live in

After God its hope alone!

See what rival machinations.

And what fierce and dire temptations

Vex us sorely every one.

HRISTMAS

Virtue unto us be given,

And demonic pride be driven

Far away from us by Thee;

To Your offspring O commend us,

Lest His brief but most tremendous

Sentence crush us utterly.

HRISTMAS

Songs of joy let us be raising

To that Savior now, in praising

Whom with us heaven's choirs delight;

News of peace from heaven is brought us,

Heaven is leagued with earth about us,

And the Church with angels bright.

God the Word, with our flesh blended,

As beforehand was intended,

She, who never knew a man,

Virgin, bears, God's temple hallowed,

Following none, by no one followed,

Ever since the world began.

That a bush with red fire gloweth,

Yet the fire no harm there doeth,

Is a new and wondrous thing:

Heaven drops dew, the clouds rain fountains.

Melt the hills and drip the mountains,

Jesse's root doth upward spring.

HRISTMAS

From that root a flower upgrows,

As the prophet plainly shows

In his prophecy of yore:

David as that root appears,

As the rod the maid that bears,

As its flower the Child she bore.

Guilty man to raise to heaven,

Condescends the God man even

To our nature's misery.

Who would not with joy be praising,

Songs of wondering gladness raising,

Grace work of such novelty?

What is more full of bliss,

What is more fathomless,

Than such a mystery?

How worthy all our praise,

How unlike human ways,

Our God's humility!

Wondrous beauty has the flower,

That rich grace's sevenfold dower

Hath commended to our care.

Let us in this flower delight us,

Which doth both by taste invite us,

And by scent and semblance rare.

HRISTMAS

Jesus, Infant death defying!

May Your birthday be supplying

Peace to us and joys divine

Flower and fruit of spotless maiden,

With immortal fragrance laden!

Glory and great praise be Thine!

CHRISTMAS

Since a Savior is born for us,

Let us, honoring Him, in chorus

Celebrate His natal day,

To us given, for us even

Born, a man 'mongst men, from heaven,

As all nations' light and stay.

Death we first from Eve inherit.

But redemption through the merit

Of the Savior's fleshly birth.

Sorrow our first parent bore us,

But the fruit, which shall restore us,

Mary with great joy brought forth.

Caring for the careless even,

God the Father looked from heaven,

Sending down His Son on earth:

In the world, yet from it hidden,

As a bridegroom, when thus bidden.

From His chamber Christ came forth.

HRISTMAS

Giant swift and giant glorious,

Giant o'er our death victorious,

Girt with power and majesty,

Came to run His course, fulfilling

All that seers had been foretelling,

And the Law's whole mystery.

Jesus, our salvation giving

Balm, Who only on all living

Peace and glory canst bestow!

Since, Your servants to deliver,

You do stoop in love, forever

All things join Your praise to show!

HRISTMAS

FASHIONED as a human creature,

Christ, His Father's image clear,

By His power, and not by nature,

Caused a Virgin's womb to bear.

No more grieving,

New songs weaving,

Let old Adam sing for mirth!

Exiles flying!

Captives lying

Prison bound! Come boldly forth!

Eve bore sadness,

But with gladness

Fruit of life a Virgin bears;

While unbroken

Still the token

Of her chastity appears.

HRISTMAS

If a crystal that is wetted

To the sun's rays be submitted,

It emits a little spark;

Neither doth the crystal break,

Neither doth this child birth take

From the maid her maiden mark.

Such begetting of a creature

Strikes experience dumb, and nature;

Reason too fails utterly;

Words could ne'er be found to show

Birth so loving, birth so low,

As at Christ's nativity.

Leaf, flower, nut, a dry rod bears.

And a maiden pure prepares

To produce God's Son Most High.

From a fleece heaven's dew shower springs;

She, He made, her Maker brings

Forth, what He had made to buy.

In the flower, leaf, nut, and shower

Mystic emblems of the power

Of the Savior's love are met.

Leaf Christ is — by shelter spreading;

Flower — by sweetness; nut — by feeding;

Dew — by grace with heaven's dew wet.

HRISTMAS

Why should it offend the Jews,

That a virgin bore a son,

When a rod could thus produce

Almonds, though a sapless one?

On the nut still let us ponder;

For, if a full light brought under,

'Tis the mystic type of light.

As it three in one appeareth,

So three gifts too it conferreth;

Unction, food, effulgence bright.

Christ the nut, — its hull His passion,

Closing round His human fashion,

And His bony frame its shell,

The incarnate Deity

And Christ's tender sympathy

In the kernel mark ye well.

Christ is light to those not seeing,

Balm, the sick from sickness freeing,

And His loving creatures' food.

O how sweet a rite! He takes

Grass — our flesh — and thereof makes

Grain for those who trust in God.

CHRISTMAS

Those, whose food You now provides,

Jesus! as 'neath rites You hides,

With Your presence satiate!

You, the Father's Co eternal

Brightness! us to joys supernal

In His glory hence translate! Amen,

CIRCUMCISION OF CHRIST

THIS festal day our Muse should be a varied

song upraising,

In strains of sweetest melody the Lord of heaven

praising.

For all things by this festival have been renewed

from heaven,

And pardon to the human race for all their misdeeds given.

The woman finds her silver piece; her candle she has lighted,

What time to flesh the mind, with God co equal, is united.

When from Jerusalem the man nigh Jericho is lying,

The good Samaritan comes by and rescues him from dying.

By clemency divine he is into the inn attended.

Whilst wine and oil, as remedy to soothe his pain, are blended.

IRCUMCISION OF CHRIST

Sweet are the balms of Him, who gives to sick men's wounds their healing,

The way of penitence for all their sinfulness revealing.

Of the two Testaments the gift of the two pennies telleth.

Since Jesus Christ, the end of both, their mysteries fulfilleth.

Lo! now the earth buds forth with dew and yet abides rainless,

Whilst bears a maid our God Himself, and is a mother stainless.

In darkness was the Infant born, Who light eternal giveth;

And circumcision on this day, the eighth day, He receiveth.

This day the Patriarchs of old foresaw in clear pre

vision,

Who gave themselves and progeny to God by circumcision.

That circumcision was performed this eighth day in a figure,

Which shall a human creature save from God's most righteous rigor.

CIRCUMCISION OF CHRIST

Ourselves, and not our foreskins, then let us be circumcising,

And cut away the lust and sin for aye within us rising.

That, cleansed in heart and flesh, to us those prizes may be given,

Which the eighth age confers on him deserving joy in heaven.

Come ye then to day here, Every organ player,

Singer and psalm sayer!

Lift your praise, And upraise,

Minstrel! your lay here! Amen.

ASTER

HAIL, great day of wondrous deeds!

Light to deepest gloom succeeds,

And to death new risen life.

Joy all sorrow triumphs o'er,

For the glory now is more

Than the former mingled strife;

Truth the shadow puts to flight,

What is new the old and trite,

Consolation tears and grief.

Hail to our new Passover;

What the Head did first secure

May each member hope to gain.

Our new Passover is Christ,

Who for us was sacrificed,

As a Lamb devoid of stain.

From the foe about our way

Christ delivers now the prey,

E'en as Samson once did say,

When the lion he slew of yore.

ASTER

David, strong in his good cause,

Rescues from the lion's claws.

And the bear's devouring jaws,

All his father's flock once more.

Samson slew the most when dying,

Jesus Christ thus typifying,

Death to Whom was victory.

Samson's name " Their Sun " declareth:

As His saints' light Christ appeareth.

Whom He shines on graciously.

From the Cross's holy transom

Flows the grapes' divinest ransom

To the well loved Church's shrine:

Round the trodden wine press thronging,

Gentile first fruits drink, with longing,

Draughts of new and gladdening wine.

Sackcloth, worn to rags and riven.

Is to royal uses given:

With sackcloth shod, see! peace does go;

The flesh has triumphed over woe.

They are from God's kingdom driven,

Who to death its king have given:

Cain has not wholly perished yet.

But for a warning sign is set.

ASTER

Though condemned once and rejected

Was this stone, it stands erected

For a trophy now, selected

As the chiefest corner stone.

Sin, not nature, He rebates,

A new creature He creates,

And Himself incorporates

Jews and Gentiles into one.

To the Head all glory be,

'Mongst the members unity! Amen.

ASTER

The Lord's own day has poured its rays,

That glorious light, the day of days;

The light of light and joy, the day

Whose glory passes not away.

This day the world's foundations laid

Distinguish, since the world was made;

On which Christ's rising from the dead

Hath new peculiar glory shed.

Ye sons of light! with lifted voice

In hope of endless joys rejoice;

And by good deeds, you members! see

That like unto your Head you be!

A holy feast this day displays,

And prayers as holy it desires;

The glory of the first of days

The first fruits of our joy requires.

EASTER

The feast of Easter's victory

The glory of all feasts must be,

'Neath many a mystic type foretold

In promise to our sires of old.

Now, rent the veil, is that well known

In the old law obscurely shown;

Fulfillment types obliterates,

And shadows light illuminates.

From what the lamb without a spot,

From what the scapegoat, typified,

Purging from us guilt's sinful blot,

The Messiah draws the veil aside.

By death deserved not doth He pay

From death deserved to set us free;

Death, seizing the unlawful prey,

Loses what was his lawfully.

That flesh, which knows nor guilt nor stain.

Destroys our guilt, the flesh's bane;

And, springing the third day again,

Doth doubting hearts' full faith maintain.

ASTER

O death of Christ, most wondrous death!

Be you in Christ our life and breath!

O death, that bows no death beneath!

Grant you to us life's glory wreath!

ASTER.

HAIL, day, the glory of all days, to thee!

Thrice happy day, Christ's day of victory!

The first day! day most fit continually

Our joy to show!

This day divine illuminates blind eyes,

Upon which Christ of hell's dark realms makes prize,

O'ercomes death and joins in one the skies

And earth below.

The judgment of the everlasting King

Hath under sin concluded everything,

That heavenly grace the weak and wavering

Might come to aid.

God's goodness and His wisdom from on high

His wrath has tempered with His clemency,

Now when all earth was being rapidly

In ruin laid.

The father of all lies, man's ancient foe,

Was trampling on us in our bitter woe,

Because no hope of pardon here below

For sin was left.

ASTER

When thus the earth despaired of cure for sin,

And silence reigned o'er it and all therein,

Forth God the Father sent His Son to men

Of hope bereft.

The insatiate robber, monster hell did bear,

Seeing the bait, but heedless of the snare,

Rushing upon the hook's point hidden there,

On it is caught;

The dignity of man, as first begun,

Is now re fashioned for us in the Son,

By Whose new resurrection to each one

Comfort is brought.

Free has He risen from depths of hell below,

Who has the human race re fashioned so,

And, on His shoulder borne. His sheep He now

To heaven does raise.

'Twixt men and angels is there perfect peace;

The ranks of heaven now swell to full increase;

Praise to the Lord Who makes wars to cease,

Eternal praise!

O let the voice of Mother Church agree

With heaven, our fatherland's, bright haraiony,

And alleluias from the faithful be

Countless to day!

ASTER

The power of death o'ercome effectually, Let us enjoy the joys of victory:

On earth be peace and jubilee on high

In heaven for aye! Amen.

ASTER

CHRIST, upon the Friday slain,

On the Sunday once again

R.ose victorious,

And those, whom He sought in love,

Gathers round Himself above,

Ever glorious.

For His faithful "people He,

Offered on the Cross's tree,

Death sustains:

To the tomb's enclosure borne,

Life once more at early mom He regains.

Christ's protection we receive

Through His Cross, if we believe,

And His Passion;

While His rising for our sakes

Possible our rising makes

From transgression.

ASTER

A sufficient sacrifice

Jesus by His death supplies

For all evil:

Through His blood, shed, cleansed are we,

And thus gain the victory

O'er the devil.

He, by dying once for all,

Freedom from death's double thrall

For us gaining.

Opens wide the gate of life,

Thereby healing all our grief

And complaining.

He, the lion strong, to day

Rising, of his powerful sway

Token shows;

For iniquity's fell lord,

He with righteousness's sword

Overthrows.

'Tis the Lord's own day, wherein

All the world, made clean from sin,

He recalls.

Whereon, death's self being slain,

And our life restored again,

Satan falls.

ASTER

Therefore from pure hearts once more

Double alleluias soar

Up to heaven;

Since away man's guilt is ta'en,

And that he shall live again

Promise given.

Jesus Christ! make You Thine own

Rise before the sun goes down

O'er creation;

May this day to all who bear

True allegiance to You here

Bring salvation!   Amen.

ASTER

SPRING'S renewal of earth's plain

New born joys to man supplies;

When the Lord doth rise again,

With Him also all things rise:

Elements upon Him wait,

Feeling, as their source, how great

Should be His solemnities.

Fires their swift flames upward throw,

Lightly the air eddies blow,

Running waters onward flow,

Earth remains unmoved below:

Light things soar above the plain,

Heavy things their place retain,

All things are renewed again.

Heights of heaven serener be,

And more tranquil grows the sea;

Breathes the air more buoyantly,

And our vale fresh verdure shows;

ASTER

What is dry once more revives,

What is cold new heat receives,

When with warmth the springtide glows.

Icy death dissolves to day;

This world's prince is borne away,

And o'er us his hateful sway

Is destroyed for evermore:

Since he in possession sought

Him in whom he had not aught,

He has lost his ancient power.

Death by life is triumphed o'er;

Man recovers now once more

All the bliss, which, lost of yore,

Paradise's joys afford:

Easy has the way there proved.

Since the cherubim removed

Thence his ever turning sword.

Christ re opens heaven again,

Loosing every captive's chain,

Bound to undergo death's pain

For his foul iniquity.

Glory for such victory won

To the Father and the Son

With the Holy Spirit be!   Amen.

ASTER

PURGE away the former leaven,

That true thanks may now be given

On the day which saw Christ rise!

Hope to us this great day yields;

Mighty is the power it wields,

As the Law's word testifies.

Egypt's sons this day were plundered;

Israel's tribes, their fetters sundered,

From the kilns were freed to day;

Servile was the occupation

Of this bound and captive nation,

Making bricks of straw and clay.

Of God's goodness let laudation,

Songs of triumph and salvation,

Burst forth now in accents clear:

This is the day the Lord Himself has made,

The day our sorrows all to rest are laid,

And which brings salvation near.

EASTER

Things to come the Law's type veileth;

Christ the promises fulfilleth,

Who doth all things consummate;

Christ's own blood, for us outpoured,

Making blunt the flaming sword,

Drives the warders from the gate.

Life's joy he, that lad, implies,

Who our laughter typifies,

In whose stead the ram was slain:

Joseph from the pit ascends,

Back to heaven His way Christ wends,

Having died His death of pain.

'Tis this serpent that devours

Pharaoh's serpents, and o'erpowers,

Scatheless, the old serpent's spite.

He provides an escape,

In a brazen serpent's shape,

From the fiery serpent's bite.

Christ the hook and thorn appeareth,

Which the serpent's jaw bone teareth:

On the cockatrice's den

When His hand this weaned child lays,

Driven off, no longer stays

That old dweller amongst men.

ASTER

Mocking children, insults throwing

At the seer to Beth el going,

Feel the bald head's righteous wrath:

David, by feigned madness stirred,

The scapegoat, the ' living bird,"

From the haunts of men flee forth.

Samson with a jaw bone slays

Thousands, and contempt displays

For a wife from 'mongst his own:

Samson Gaza's bolts unfastens,

And, its gates uplifting, hastens

With them to the mountain's crown.

Judah's lion by this token

Boldly, death's dread portals broken,

Rises the third day once more:

Back to Heaven rich fruits of daring

To our mother's bosom bearing.

When He hears the Father's roar.

Jonah, from his duty flying,

Three days in her belly lying,

Our true Jonah typifying,

Does the whale restore alive.

ASTER

Clustered camphire fresh life shows

Spreads abroad and larger grows:

Blight alone the Law's bud knows,

And the Church doth bloom and thrive.

Death and life's long strife is ended!

Christ has risen indeed, attended

By a witness crowd, ascended

With Him, who His glory show.

Morning new, morn gladness reaping!

Wipe away our eve of weeping;

Life o'er death is triumph keeping,

'Tis the time for joyance now!

Jesus Victor, life bestowing!

Jesus, Way to true life going!

Through Your death death's self o'erthrowing!

At Your Paschal feast o'erflowing

Grant us in full trust a place!

Bread of life and Water living!

Vine, the tnie Vine, much fruit giving!

Feed us, cleanse us from sin's striving.

That, at second death arriving,

We escape it through Your grace! Amen.

SCENSION

SATAN and the realms infernal

Having spoiled, to joys supernal

Christ returns back once more:

As His upward way He wends,

As before, when He descends,

Angels set them to adore.

As above the stars He goes,

Here no more Himself He shows,

Bodily, to mortal sight;

But all rule to Him is given,

Who is with His Sire in Heaven

One in majesty and might.

Victor now, from perils warded,

He in heaven has been accorded

Empire over all therein;

Nevermore shall He be dying,

Nevermore through death supplying

Means to purify man's sin.

ASENCION

Once for all He took our nature,

Once He suffered, once, a creature,

Was for sin content to die:

Further pain shall He know never,

But, in perfect peace for ever.

Compass endless joys on high.

Thus He spoke, as He ascended;

These things straitly He commanded.

And impressed upon His own:

" Go through all the world and preach ye.

Every nation therein teach ye

Both by word and wonder done.

" For I go unto My Father,

To return, as ye may gather,

Since shall come a Comforter,

Who shall make you bold and fearless,

Of all consequences careless,

Eloquent in speech and clear.

" Those laid low by sickness on them.

When ye lay your hands upon them.

Shall their former health regain:

All things hurtful and annoying,

With all deadly snakes, destroying,

Ye shall drive out plagues and pain.

ASCENSION

"Whosoever but believes,

And with simple faith receives

Baptism's sure remedy,

Shall be cleansed from all transgression,

And have with the saints possession

Of eternal joys on high! " Amen.

PENTECOST

DAY delightful! day most noted!

When o'er Christ's disciples floated

Fire sent from the throne on high,

Filling hearts and tongues endowing,

And on hearts and tongues bestowing

Words and thoughts in harmony!

Christ, as once His word had spoken,

Sent His spouse a pledge and token,

Coming back the fiftieth day.

After streams of honey sweet

Oil that rock poured forth from it,

Which is now man's firmest stay.

From the mount to Jewry came

God's law, not in tongues of flame,

But on tables wrought from stone:

In a furnished upper room.

Given but to few, there come

Hearts renewed, and tongues as one.

ENTECOST

O the joy and jubilation

Of that day, when first foundation

Of the early Church was laid:

When the Church, then first begun,

Souls three thousand to it won,

Lively first fruits of it made.

Thus one faith binds earth's two nations,

Like the early dispensation's

Twofold offering of bread:

The Head Corner stone two races

By His presence interlaces.

And thus one the two are made.

In new bottles, not in olden.

Must the new made wine be holden:

Brings the widow but the cruse;

Oil is by Elijah given:

So doth God for dew from heaven

Hearts, if fitting vessels, use.

Of this wine or oil before Thee,

Of this dew, are we unworthy,

If we have not peace within:

Not in hearts 'gainst God rebelling,

Can this Comforter be dwelling.

Nor in those made dark through sin.

PENTECOST

Come, You Comforter benign!

Rule our hearts and tongues, Divine!

Gall or poison, where You shine,

May not any more be found:

There is not a joy or pleasure,

Health and rest are not a treasure,

Nothing is sweet, all scant in measure,

Where Your grace does not abound.

You, for light and unction given,

A sweet savor sent from heaven,

Fills simple water even

With a new mysterious power:

We, re made by Your creation,

Give You, with pure hearts, laudation;

Sons of grace, by generation

Sons of wrath who were before.

You, Who are both gift and giver,

Helping every good endeavor,

Cause our hearts to praise You ever.

And our lips, O let us never

But in blessing You employ:

Wash out every evil passion.

Who alone canst purge transgression!

And in Christ our souls refashion,

That we may, in full possession.

Our new nature's bliss enjoy!   Amen.

PENTECOST

Comforter, from both together,

From the Son and from the Father,

Who proceeds equally!

Eloquent our utterance render;

With Your splendor

Bright engender

In our hearts true warmth for Thee.

Love of Father, Son, together;

Equal of them both; with either

One: the same in every part! lo

All You fill, all You lovest,

Stars You rule, heaven You movest,

Though immovable You are.

Light the dearest!

Light the clearest!

Off You scarest,

As You nearest,

ENTECOST

From the heart its gloomy night:

All the pure You purifiest,

You it is that sin destroyest,

And its mildew's baleful blight.

Knowledge of the truth You spreadest;

On the way of peace You leadest,

And the path of righteousness

From You thrusting

Hearts unruly,

You all trusting

Hearts and holy

Dost with gifts of wisdom bless.

When You teachest,

Nothing obscure is!

Where You reachest,

Nothing impure is;

And, if present You wilt be.

Hearts in You then buthely glory,

And the conscience joys before Thee,

Gladdened, purified, by Thee.

Elements their mystic dower,

Sacraments their saving power,

But through You alone possess

ENTECOST

What can harm us You repel,

You expose and You quell,

Adversaries' wickedness.

Where You light,

Hearts are bright;

Gloom enshrouded

Clouds that brooded

There, before You disappear;

Fire all holy!

Hearts You truly

Never burn,

But there yearn.

When You come, cares to clear.

You the heart, experience needing,

Languor pleading,

Little heeding,

Dost instruct and rouse to right;

Speeches framing, tongues endowing,

And bestowing

Love all glowing,

Hearts You make in good delight.

PENTECOST

Only refuge of the poor!

Give us scorn for things terrestrial,

And to care for things celestial

Lead our longings more and more!

Comfort wholly,

Founder solely,

Inmate truly.

Lover throughly,

Of those hearts that bow to Thee!

Concord, where is discord, raising,

Ills thence chasing,

Guilt effacing,

Bring us true security!

You, Who once by visitation

Did inform, and consolation

To Your scared disciples give!

Deign You now to come unto us:

If it please You, comfort show us,

And all nations that believe!

One excelling

Greatness sharing,

One as well in

Power appearing,

ENTECOST

But one God three Persons are.

Coming forth from two together,

You co equal are with either,

No disparity is there.

Such as is the Father You are;

Since so great and such You now are,

By Your servants unto Thee,

With the Sire, and Son, in heaven

Our Redeemer, praise be given,

As is due, most reverently!   Amen.

ENTECOST

AY the Spirit on us shine,

One in essence all divine,

Septiform in gifts of grace!

May His beams from Heaven's height

Flood the darkened heart with light

And our lusts' ensnaring ways!

First the penal Law came, clouded

O'er with types, in mystery shrouded,

Ere the Gospel light shone forth.

'Neath the foliage of the letter lo

May the spirit, free from fetter,

Of that Gospel spread o'er earth!

From the Mount the Law was given

Unto all; new grace from Heaven

In a chamber to a few;

The position of which places

Brings out the respective graces

Of their laws and gifts to view.

ENTECOST

Flames of fire, the trump's loud sound,

Din and darkness all around,

Bickering lightnings sent abroad,

Strike wild terror to the heart,

Nor the fostering love impart,

Which that unction has outpoured.

Thus were given

Out of heaven

Laws to sinners from the Mount;

Laws of terror,

Chastening error,

Making love of small account.

By the fathers, pre elected,

God like works are now effected;

They unloose sin's galling bond:

Rain their words, their threatenings thunder,

With their words their works of wonder,

New and startling, correspond.

Caring for each sickly creature,

They condemn disease, not nature;

Punishing iniquity,

Sinners they strike down and chasten;

Chains they loosen, chains they fasten,

With a power from limit free.

ENTECOST

Like a Jubilee appeareth

The appearance this day weareth,

If its mystery you would'st know;

When three thousand souls make haste

'Amongst believers to be classed,

And the Church doth thrive and grow.

"Jubilee " is a provision

Made for change or for remission,

Freely to their first condition

Calling those in misery.

May the law, by love enacted,

Freeing us, by sin distracted,

Make us, to its gifts attracted,

Fit for perfect liberty! Amen.

PENTECOST

The Spirit dear,

That Comforter,

Who, before all ages were,

By procession came from God,

On a race,

That sought His face,

Striving for His saving grace,

Hath the kiss of peace bestowed.

On this day,

When its first ray

The third hour doth display,

Comes full pardon's gift so bright,

Which is then

For all their sin

Freely offered to all men

By the Father of all light.

Its bright sheen

Was fully seen.

And inspired bold dauntless men

ENTECOST

With a sweet refreshment there;

Yea, did tame

With rushing flame,

And instruct and teach the same

In its learning rich and rare.

Men, before

Devoid of lore.

Weak and frail, and lacking power

Through the lack of eloquence,

Useful prove,

Friends worthy love,

And beloved where'er they move,

Through the grace it doth dispense.

Feelingly,

Not fearfully,

Thus would true benignity

To its well beloved come:

Instantly

Sin's infamy

Never failing charity

Would wipe off us and consume.

O mine ear

With joy doth hear.

PENTECOST

That, whene'er His help is near,

Such untold felicity

We shall meet with bounding feet ...

Let all avarice vanish hence,

Far away, wrong doing! flee:

No more pride and insolence.

No more infidelity!

Let the truth still hold its place,

And let but humility

Search the conscience, — grace for grace, —

With all meekness modestly.

May the All in All so bless

Christ the Lord's own family,

That it, marked by holiness,

Be from ills forever free!

Let the truth there hold its place,

Let it sin ne'er understand:

Let its brightness never cease

In the heavenly fatherland! Amen.

ENTECOST

Come, our comfort's chief reviver!

Hope of saving health, Life giver!

May Your grace here present be!

Pleasant heat, dew from above!

Outgrowth from the God of love!

One with it substantially!

Who from both proceeds, neither

Canst be separate from either,

Linked with both of them together

By an everlasting tie;

Dew and breath of both in heaven!

By both Sire and Son be given

Of Your Spirit to us even

In rich plenty from on high.

Of this dew and breath you hearest;

Deem Him scent too, whereby clearest

Is His Godhead to us shown.

PENTECOST

As this dew, that from it bursts,

Tastes man more, the more he thirsts

With a thirst that nothing tones down.

For the world's regeneration

It to water consecration

Gave, on which at the creation,

O'er its surface borne, it sate.

Fountain, source of love's devotion!

Fountain, cleansing sinful motion!

Fountain from the Godhead's ocean,

That all founts does consecrate!

Fire, unfed by fuel, flowing

From the rod with ardent glowing

That devours both kid and bread!

Fire, unlike all fire, O may the

Altar of our soul, we pray Thee,

Ever with Your flame be fed!

Darkly by the women seven

Are You figured, Truth of Heaven!

Inner life to all things given!

Spirit, Sevenfold in grace!

You all various types betoken,

Though Your oneness be unbroken;

Nor of You may it be spoken,

That a type can You embrace.

ENTECOST

Fire of life and life's bright river!

Cleanse and fertilize hearts ever,

Giving grace in everything;

Touched with fire of true love, take us

To You, and in mercy make us

Holiness's offering!

Sire and Son's blest emanation

Be from sin our restoration,

When worn out, our sustentation,

And our comfort, when we mourn!

Love both pure and noble truly!

Heat that warms, but ne'er unduly!

May Your unction heal those throughly,

Who with unchaste ardor burn!

Voice, that doth no sounds deliver!

Still small voice, that whispers ever,

Saints inspiring to endeavor!

Voice of joy and sweetness! never

Cease to sound within our heart!

Light, away all falsehood driving!

Light, to truth incentive giving!

Grant that— life, health, thence deriving,

Of Your brightness ever living

All of us may have our part! Amen.

RINITY

O the Trine God, not Gods three,

The Trinity in Unity,

Let the Church now bow the knee!

All creation

Indication,

Clear and lucid, gives of a Trinity.

Let the sober mind up to God then rise!

Of the Father and of the Son,

With the Paraclete Spirit one.

To our eyes

May God's grace reveal all the mysteries!

There are Persons three, and many

Mysteries marking these Persons distinctively:

One by nature, all and any,

Neither is separately less than all the three.

Equal in all Three is knowledge, power, and will.

Yet in their three Persons is there difference still:

— Equal reverence to the Three,

To the One all glory, be! Amen.

RINITY

WE, the Unity confessing,

Must the Trinity be blessing

In our worship equally;

In three Persons thus believing;

Difference 'between them each perceiving

In their Personality.

Relatively of these speak we,

Substantively but one make we.

Nor three Persons in them see;

Call them three or threefold, never

But one substance are they ever.

Neither in their essence three.

One in being, One in power,

One in will and wisdom's dower,

One in all respects they be:

Of all these three Persons, either

One, or two, or all together.

Are Almighty equally.

RINITY

Father, Son, and Spirit Holy,

Are one God, but each has truly

Some peculiar property:

One their goodness, one their might, is;

One their glory', one their light, is;

One are they entirely.

Equal are the Son and Father,

But from this we may not gather

That their Persons are the same:

One with Son and Father either,

Not from one, but both together.

The connecting Spirit came.

These three Persons that we mention

Are beyond man's comprehension,

As the difference each one shows:

Time and place alike unbounded

Are for them, and unsurrounded

By the limits nature knows.

Naught but God God's self comprises,

Nor from other cause arises,

Cause of all causality:

Though the cause, all things respecting,

Formal, final, and effecting,

Immaterial is He.

TRINITY

To describe these Persons duly

Far transcends man's reason truly,

And exceeds his wit as well:

What that birth is, that procession,

Though faith doubts not, my confession

Must be that I cannot tell.

Who believes this, nothing dismays

He ne'er ignorantly strays

From this creed's right royal road;

Keeps the faith, his life makes purer,

Not declining into error

Censured by the Church of God.

In this faith then let us glory,

And in one consistent story

Hold it in its verity:

Praise be to the Triune Godhead;

To the Three in One included

Co eternal glory be! Amen.

DEDICATION OF A CHURCH

O HOW LOVELY ARE THE COURTS DIVINE OF THE

LORD OF HOSTS, HIS HALLOWED SHRINE!

O HOW skilled the

Hands that build thee;

How secure thy walls remain;

Ne'er subverted,

But supported

Rather by wind, flood, and rain!

O how comely thy foundations,

By deep mysteries' celebrations

Shadowing forth the coming day!

Adam, when in sleep reclining,

From his side pours Eve, beginning

Thus a bond to last for aye.

Noah, in ark of wood constructed.

O'er that flood is safe conducted,

Which did all the world destroy.

DEDICATION OF A CHURCH

Great with offspring long awaited,

Aged Sarah laughs, elated.

Giving milk to feed our joy.

Thirst the servant legate slakes,

And its fill his camel takes,

From Rebecca's water pail.

She, as rings and chains she wears,

Fitly thus herself prepares

To assume the bridal veil.

Since it so the letter vaunteth,

Jacob now the Law supplanteth.

Whilst it roams forth far and wide.

Rachel, since she sees much hidden

From Leah's tender sight, is bidden

To an equal rank as bride.

Tamar, long a widow biding,

By the way her features hiding,

Doth twin sons to Judah bear.

Here in basket made of rushes

Moses see, who, while she washes,

Was perceived by maiden fair.

Here the male lamb, immolated,

Wherewith Israel's tribes are sated.

And besprinkled with its blood.

EDICATION OF A CHURCH

Here the Red Sea, safe passed over,

Which the Egyptian host did cover

With its deep devouring flood.

Here the pot that manna fills;

Here the Decalogue God wills,

In the ark of covenant bound.

Here the Temple's decorations;

Aaron's robes for ministrations,

Chief the one' that sweeps the ground.

Here his wife Uriah loses;

Here the king for consort chooses

Bathsheba, his throne to share.

As she by him takes her station,

Dons she gold's rich decoration,

Such as monarchs' daughters wear.

Here Sheba's queen progresses,

She, whom Solomon impresses

With his wisdom all divine:

Black she is, but comely; blending

Charms, as when in smoke ascending

Myrrh and frankincense combine.

Things forth coming,

Darkly looming.

EDICATION OF A CHURCH

'Neath types shaded,

Are paraded

Plainly by this day of grace:

With the dear one

Lying near one,

Rest we, raising

Psalms of praising

For the marriage now takes place.

On first assembling for the feast

Is heard the trumpets' thrilling blast;

Sweet psalteries' notes ring forth at last.

The Bridegroom in ten thousand ways

These myriad minstrels hymn, whose lays

Are still the same, as still they raise

Their Alleluia's endless praise!

EDICATION OF A CHURCH

SOLOMON, the King, a Temple

Built, whose pattern and example

Christ, with Holy Church, appears:

He, its founder and foundation,

Sway, through grace's mediation,

As the Church's ruler bears.

Squarely built, this Temple's bases

Are of marble; each wall's space is

Formed of stones cut evenly:

Chastity's fair flower there twines;

Each squared stone therein combines,

Prelates' nerve and constancy.

Its far reaching

Length, and stretching

Width, and height that tempts the sky,

Faith explaining

The true meaning,

Are Faith, Hope, and Charity.

DEDICATION OF A CHURCH

Tripartite is this fair Temple,

After the Triune's example,

With first, third, and middle floor:

First, the living signifying;

Second, those in death now lying.

Third, those raised to life once more.

All the parts together rated,

Or alone, are calculated

Threescore cubits wide to be:

Triply do these three, thus blending,

Harmonize with the transcending

Trinity in Unity.

Gorgeous ritual

And perpetual

Scents, sweet smelling.

Fill God's dwelling.

Cassia, myrrh, and cinnamon;

Signifying

Never dying

Christian graces,

Prayers, and praises,

Grateful offerings at His throne.

In this palace

Is each chalice

EDICATION OF A CHURCH

A gold measure

From the treasure

Pre elected secretly:

For all teachers'

Minds, and preachers',

Thoroughly furnished.

Purged, and burnished.

By the Spirit's fire should be.

Thus with treasure,

David's pleasure

Had collected.

Is erected

Solomon's great sanctuary;

But the dwelling,

All excelling,

Timber sending,

Craftsmen lending,

Tyre's are fashioned cunningly.

Formed of Jew and Gentile races,

Builds the Church her holy places.

As did both the Temple raise.

Christ, Who both in one unitest!

Comer stone of each! the brightest

Glory be to You and praise. Amen.

DEDICATION OF A CHURCH

Let our choir now loudly join their Alleluia's brightest strains,

The eternal Monarch praising, who o'er all creation reigns!

Unto Him the universal Church unites us in love,

Like a shining ladder reaching to the heights of heaven above.

To His honor psalms of gladness we in tuneful strains upraise,

Paying thus the proper tribute to Him of our daily praise.

O hall of bliss! where, in due order,

Troops of angels gather continually;

And with divine words, alternating.

Join sweet strains of ravishing melody! lo

EDICATION OF A CHURCH

'Tis the home of which the former Testament did sound the praise,

And of which the New declares that 'tis Christ Himself that says:

"Seeing I have chosen this to be my throne of purity,

Henceforth through undying ages here my resting place shall be! "

Tower! on a Mount erected,

And with cement that melts not upon it founded,

By perennial walls protected,

And with pillared gold surrounded,

Of divers jewels, polished with fine skill, compounded,

For their rarity selected!

Elect Mother! hail! whom, blessing,

Christ is in these words addressing

Of impassioned prophecy:

" Rise, my lovely spouse! the fairest

'Mongst earth's daughters you appearest,

Brighter than the sun on high!

" Lo! thy head is like Mount Carmel,

And the flowing locks upon it, as with regal purple,

red:

DEDICATION OF A CHURCH

Doves' eyes do thine eyes resemble;

Like a piece of a pomegranate are the temples of

thine head.

"Like a column is thy neck and like an ivory

tower's walls;

Milk and honey 'neath thy tongue, thy lips a

comb whence honey falls."

Therefore still with us, the servants

Of Your spouse, O Christ! we pray You, in Your

never failing love

Kindly deign You to be present:

Everywhere with Your salvation visit us from heaven

above!

Through her mediation also, King Most High!

Perpetually,

We implore Thee

Loudly, that with alleluias we 'midst joys of Paradise

May adore Thee!

DEDICATION OF A CHURCH

JERUSALEM and Sion's daughters fair!

J And all the faithful crowd that worship there!

That ceaseless strain of tuneful joy prepare,

" Alleluia! "

For Christ, Who does all righteousness display,

Is to our Mother Church espoused to day,

That Church, whom He in love has drawn away

From depths of woe.

Through the blest Spirit's mercy from above

The Bride rejoices in the Bridegroom's love:

Earth's queens with glorious praises doth she move

To call her blest.

*Mid greater joy still is her dowry given:

What! and how great! that threefold power, which

heaven,

And earth below, and the dread judgments even

Of hell affects.

Belief is wise, though strange my tale: that bride,

By gifts of such vast magnitude allied

To Him, was taken out of His own side

By the God Man

EDICATION OF A CHURCH

That thus the Church should form and shape receive

In equal glory, we a type believe

Was woman, formed — source of our sorrow, Eve! —

From Adam's rib.

Eve a stepmother has been to her seed;

The Church to her elect a mother indeed.

Life's haven, an asylum in their need,

And sure defence.

She, beautiful and great, in birth divine,

Fair as the moon, clear as the sun doth shine;

More terrible than armies' serried line.

With banners dight.

Multifold is she, yet but one alone;

As all together, and each singly, known;

Of every age and sex, yet only one;

Troops she brings forth.

Jordan! thy waves a type of her appear.

And she, that from the ends of earth drew near,

That, face to face, she might the wisdom hear

Of Solomon.

She, whom these types, when understood, portray,

Robed for her marriage feast in bright array,

Presides o'er all the heavenly host to day,

The bride of Christ.

DEDICATION OF A CHURCH

O holy joy's bright feast day in the skies,

Which joins the Church with Christ in marriage ties!

That marriage day, whose rite mankind allies

With saving health!

O happy gathering! O sweet feast of heaven!

When consolation to the lapsed is given,

And to the sinner, to despair now driven,

A breathing space!

Here their rewards are to the righteous paid,

And angels' joys, renewed again, displayed;

Feast, by the grace of charity thus made

Too full of joy!

The fount of wisdom from the first has known,

Through the clear insight given by grace alone,

As the due course of things has onward gone,

What is to be:

Therefore may Christ, by these His marriage rites,

Make us, refreshed thereby with true delights.

Partake those joys to which His love invites

All His elect. Amen.

T. ANDREW

LET us, shouts of gladness raising,

Now delighted to be praising

The Apostle Andrew be:

Whose faith, life, and doctrine precious,

With his mighty works for Jesus,

Should be honored worthily.

He, who first the true light's glowing

Saw, at John the Baptist's showing,

Peter led the faith to see!

Then are Peter and his brother

Called along with one another

At the Sea of Galilee.

Fishermen till then, both preachers

Of the word become and teachers

Of the rules of righteousness

Now a net to catch men loose they,

And a wary forethought use they

The young Church to guard and bless.

T. ANDREW

Andrew soon his brother leaves,

When commission he receives,

And is in Achaia placed:

Of which province a great part,

By God's grace convinced in heart,

To the nets of Andrew haste.

By his faith, life, signs, and speeches

This great, good, man's doctrine reaches

And reforms the people's heart.

When Aegeans finds out

All that Andrew thus had wrought.

Forth his bitter wrath stings start.

His staid heart and manly spirit,

Who in this life saw no merit,

Stronger from endurance grow.

Flattering or tormenting either.

His insensate judge by neither

Can his strength of mind overthrow.

When he sees the cross preparing.

Like his Master, suffering sharing,

The disciple longs to be;

For Christ's death he pays his own,

And for its triumphal crown

On the cross seeks eagerly.

T. ANDREW

Upon the cross he lived two days,

Thenceforth to live in heaven always;

Nor, when the people wished, would he

Be lifted from the fatal tree.

Nigh half an hour upon that height

Bathed in a Height exceeding bright,

In light, exulting at the sight,

He passes to the halls of light.

Andrew, crowned with endless glory!

Rich in prayer propitiatory!

Of whose brilliant death the story

Tis so sweet in thought to trace!

From this vale of woe exceeding

To that light such radiance shedding.

Loving shepherd, spirits feeding!

O transport us by thy grace! Amen.

T. NICHOLAS

LET us all exult together, as with one united voice

We upon his solemn feast day 'in St. Nicholas rejoice;

Who, whilst in his cradle lying, by observing duly fast,

Heavenly joys began to merit even at his mother's breast.

In his youth he chooses letters, that his study they may be,

To all evil lust a stranger, from all sinful passions free.

This blest confessor, Whom, as worthy of the office, 'twas a voice from heaven praised,

Thereby exalted, Amongst bishops to the very highest rank is forth with raised.

ST. NICHOLAS

There was too in his character benevolence exceeding,

And many a bounty he bestowed, the tale of sorrow

heeding.

With gold he saved some maidens, who had else

vile lives been leading,

Relieving all their father's want, when help most

sorely needing.

Certain sailors once, when sailing,

And fighting 'gainst fierce waves with struggles

unavailing.

Shipwrecked nigh through stress of weather;

Hope of life already failing,

Amid such dangers set, aloud their fate bewailing.

Lift their voices altogether:

" Blessed Nicholas! O steer us

From the straits of death so near us

To the haven of the sea!

To that harbor in the distance

Draw us, who does grant assistance

Through the grace of charity!

" Lo! " — while thus they cried, nor vainly,

" I am here! " a voice said plainly,

ST. NICHOLAS

" To watch o'er you and to aid! "

Instantly blow favoring breezes,

Instantly the tempest ceases,

And to rest the sea is laid.

We, now in this world abiding,

Have been wrecked, as we were riding

O'er the deep abyss of vice:

Draw us, Nicholas most glorious!

To the home of peace victorious,

To the port of Paradise!

From his tomb, to heal diseases,

Oil abundant flows forth,

Which the sick from pain releases

Through his prayers' availing worth.

May we of the self same ointment

Through thy pious prayer to God Gain possession,

Which did by the Lord's appointment

Heal the wounds of Mary's load

Of transgression!

Let them joy throughout all ages, who observe this

holy day,

And, when this life's course is ended, crowned in heaven by Christ be they!

Amen! let all creatures say!

T. STEPHEN

Yesterday the world, elated,

Joyed, and, joying, celebrated

Christ the Savior's natal day:

Yesterday, heaven's King surrounding,

Angel choirs, his welcome sounding,

Sang to him with joyful lay.

Protomartyr and a deacon,

Faith's clear light and life's bright beacon,

For his wonder works well known,

Stephen on this day all glorious

Won the victory, and, victorious,

Trod the unbelievers down.

Thus, since those 'gainst light engaging.

Conquered, fail, behold them raging

Like wild beasts in their despair:

Lying Avitnesses they bring.

And with bitter words they sting,

Seed of vipers that they are!

T. STEPHEN

Champion! yield to none, but ever

Persevere in your endeavor,

Stephen! sure of sure reward:

Their false witnesses withstand,

And confute all Satan's band

By your eloquence outpoured.

In the heavens thy Witness dwells;

Truly, faithfully. He tells

How you have no evil done:

Since "a crown" for name you bears,

Suffering first you fitly shares,

Till your glory crown be won.

For that crown's unfading dower

Choose to bear brief torture's power;

There awaits thee victory!

Death new birth for thee portends,

And its pain, which quickly ends,

Is the dawn of life to thee.

Full of the blest Spirit's grace,

Stephen into heaven's space

Penetrates with lightened eyes;

Gazing on God's glory, he

Waxes strong for victory,

Longing for its deathless prize.

 *T. STEPHEN*

Lo! At God's own right hand standing,

Jesus, in thy cause contending,

Stephen! lift your eyes and see!

Cry that heaven now open lies;

And that Christ your eye descries

Cry aloud in accents free!

To his Lord his soul commending,

Sweet he deems it at life's ending

'Neath these stones for him to fall.

Saul stands by and keeps the clothes

Of each stoner as he throws,

Stoning Stephen through them all

That the Lord would not be laying

To his murderers' charge this slaying,

Stephen kneels down, and, praying,

Mourns their mad and reckless deed:

So asleep in Christ fell Stephen,

Who had Christ to serve so striven,

And now lives with Christ in heaven,

First fruits of the martyrs' seed!

That in Africa from death

He six men to life revived.

Is a fact Augustine saith,

And one commonly believed.

T. STEPHEN

When, by God's grace, his remains

From their grave to light were brought,

Then were given heavy rains

On the earth in time of drought.

He by perfume rare alone

Makes disease and demons flee,

And due praise and fame has won

With a deathless memory.

Martyr! whose sweet name doth live

In the Church so pleasantly,

An enfeebled world revive

With thy heavenly fragrancy! Amen.

T. STEPHEN

LO! A rose, new odor shedding,

Bright with beauty, all exceeding,

From the halls of heaven,

Out of Egypt is invited,

And to follow Christ delighted,

After witness given.

An unhappy, evil nation

Treats its victim's self oblation

In unworthy fashion,

And Christ's truths, for which he pleads;

Though therefrom he ne'er recedes

Through his fiery passion.

In his bruised flesh he rejoices;

Bent his knee and soft his voice is,

For the Jews' race pleading,

That 'gainst them his causeless passion

Be not charged, of their transgression

Being thus unheeding.

T. STEPHEN

His hope's certain expectation

Is confirmed to demonstration,

When he Christ perceiveth

In His Father's glory standing;

On the rock then, safe contending,

Awe struck foes he driveth.

As a grape, the wine press feeding,

Would have wine pressed thence by treading,

Lest it useless seems;

So the martyr stoning pleases.

Knowing his reward increases,

As his life blood streams.

Let us, through earth's desert driven

Here and there, to follow Stephen

In his course endeavor;

That, safe such a leader under.

We the Triune's true light yonder

May enjoy for ever! Amen.

*T JOHN THE EVANGELIST*

ON his feast with gratulation

Joy we at John's exaltation,

As we pay our public vows!

Let the mouth so sing his praises,

That the relish which it raises

The glad heart may never lose.

This is he most loved by Jesus,

Who drank draughts of wisdom precious,

As he on His breast did lean:

To whom Mary was commended

From Christ's cross; who, virgin, tended

Her who had not known a man.

Inwardly with warm love glowing,

Outwardly bright virtue showing,

Eloquence and wonders wrought;

As by lust's consuming fever.

So by tortures' heat, touched never,

From the oil vat came he out.

T JOHN THE EVANGELIST

Poison's strength he overpowered,

Death, disease, beneath him cowered,

And the very devils too:

But the man, such power possessing,

Could no less bring health and blessing

Unto those in want and woe.

Broken gems by him were mended,

And their value was expended

On the poor, his pious loan.

He produces boundless treasure,

Who from tree twigs at his pleasure

Fashioned gold, and gems from stone.

By a friend to banquet bidden,

Christ, I mean, no longer hidden,

Seen with His disciples there,

From the grave, where he was lying.

He arose in form undying,

In the heavenly feast to share.

There are crowds to testify.

Nay, yourself may trust your eye,

How that, where he once did lie,

Flows forth manna, a supply

From the table of the Lord.

T JOHN THE EVANGELIST

As he doth his Gospel write,

Eagle like in upward flight,

He beholds the Light of Light,

Its primeval source, to wit,

" In the beginning was the Word! "

A perverse and heathen nation,

All of Asia's population,

To the faith his wonders won.

Illustrated by his writing,

Unity, the Church uniting,

Firmer ground now stands upon.

Vessel, hail! that no sin stains!

Vessel, that heaven's dew contains! Which within quite pure remains,

Bright without, all dignity!

Cause us, like thee, to be holy,

And, with spirits chastened throughly,

Let us see the Godhead fully,

In one substance Persons three. Amen.

T JOHN THE EVANGELIST

JOHN'S theology declareth,

Though on earth all flesh appeareth

To decline in swift decay,

That the Word's word self existent,

Through all ages still consistent,

Will remain nor pass away.

As the loved disciple sinks

On his Master's breast, and drinks

Wisdom's fount and learning's stream.

From a posture so endearing

Word and faith, and speech and hearing,

Mind and God, converging seem.

By the flights of thought thence taken,

Flesh and carnal sense forsaken,

Far o'er error's cloudy night,

His Eagle like, by observation,

The true Sun's illumination,

Keeps his keen eyed heart in sight.

T JOHN THE EVANGELIST

Want of Style the sense confuses,

But such subtlety John uses,

And so Catholic his faith,

That all heretics, depraving

Doctrines of that Word soul saving.

Fail to gainsay aught he saith.

Lo! that Word, beyond expression,

Who all very good did fashion

By His power of creation,

From the eternal Sire appears

Undivided, John declares,

Save in Personal relation.

Whom with chaste milk Matthew feeds,

Which from virgin breasts proceeds,

With much toil and trouble blended

Whom that ox horn, Luke's pen, places

On the cross and high upraises,

As the serpent was suspended;

Whom from death's sepulchral portal

Lion Mark restores immortal.

Whilst earth quakes and rocks are riven;

Him John paints with skill unstudied,

First and last, God in true Godhead,

Father of all earth and heaven.

ST JOHN THE EVANGELIST

He the eyes all round these creatures,

Their swift wings, their fourfold features,

And the wheels that stand beside them,

In their might had seen in heaven,

Ere form here to them was given,

Or the charioteer to guide them.

They describe what craft Christ suffered;

Violence by Pilate offered,

With the thorn crown, then endured:

He, borne up on soaring pinion,

Treats of Christ's supreme dominion,

And of His avenging sword.

On his wings, though uninstructed,

Rise the King's own wheels, conducted

As though on the living four;

While the heavenly harpers, kneeling

At the Father's throne, their thrilling

Alleluia's song outpour! Amen,

ST JOHN THE EVANGELIST

LET our choir upon this day, — as they lift

their anthem, pay, — Christ due praises;

Day, when John became a guest — at high heaven's

supernal feast — with his brethren;

Who for marvels by him done, — many and most

great, was known, — whilst here living;

Father, vessel, marriage bed — and himself he left,

instead — Christ to follow.

More illustrious than the rest — lying upon Jesus'

breast — at the supper;

From the Cross to this chaste one — was the Virgin

by the Son — given over.

Boiling oil he overcame, — and, when shorn for

scoff and shame, — mocked their scourgings;

For the Gospel's honor spent, — banishment he

underwent, — torture, fetters.

T JOHN THE EVANGELIST

He through faith did poison drain, — and the dead

revived again, — first restoring a young man,

— then a mother.

Gold from foliage fashioned he, — out of pebbles

jewelry, — and their fragments perfectly

put together.

lo Christ visits him to call him home, — and he, alive

still, entereth the tomb, — thence seeks heaven.

Now, Christ! to You plead voice and prayer,

bring us to be his partners there, — through

the ages! Amen.

T JOHN THE EVANGELIST

Preface. John, the eagle, first of Evangelists, the

Triune God revealeth!

BLESSED resting place of grace!

Who on heaven's great King does gaze

With the mind's eye, face to face,

All unblinded!

For the Spirit shows God's throne

To him, deifying John,

Making him with angels one,

Heavenly minded!

Now the water, life supplying,

As it springs up, drinks he, lying

On the bosom of the Lord:

Now he shines with many a wonder,

Now the force of fire keeps under,

And of hot oil round him poured.

Wondrous it seems to be,

That, 'mid torture's agony.

T JOHN THE EVANGELIST

Martyrdom one should gain,

And yet never feel the pain.

O martyr! O virgin! — that Virgin's guardian,

— who did earth's chief Glory bear!

From Whom is, in Whom is, — through Whom is

everything, — may He through thee hear our

prayer!

O you, beloved above the rest!

Ask Christ, Who loved thee far the best,

To Him pressing

Prayers addressing,

For His reconciling grace,

River! lead us to the fountain;

Hill! conduct us to the mountain;

Who endurest

Virgin purest!

Let us see the Bridegroom's face.

Conclusion, To the Bridegroom endless praise!

T. *THOMAS OF CANTERBURY*

JOY, O Sion! and rejoice thou;

With both vow and lifted voice now,

With a holy joy be glad!

For Christ's sake, assassinated,

Is thy Thomas immolated,

A most precious victim made.

Primate, legate, though created.

He was ne'er with pride elated

By his honors' lofty height;

Steward of the King of heaven,

He was into exile driven,

Since he for his flock would fight.

With the Spirit's sword girt round him,

Victory with full triumph crowned him.

As with pastoral spear he fought;

For his God's law to be fighting,

For his flock's sake death inviting,

Ever was his chiefest thought.

T. THOMAS OF CANTERBURY

Losing then its guide and master,

And deprived thus of its pastor,

Canterbury deeply grieved;

But then one, so justly noted,

Sens in France, with joy devoted.

And with glad acclaim received.

In his absence sore prostrated,

And, when prostrate, violated.

Was the Church no longer free;

So from 'mongst us you departed,

Father! but aside ne'er started

From the path of probity.

Once, amid the courtier bevy,

You wast foremost of the levy

In the palace of the king;

All the people approbation,

And the world loud acclamation,

As its wont is, offering.

Well timed was thy transformation;

For of thee thy consecration

By a blest reciprocation

Made a new man happily:

You thine opposition ended.

As a wall, the Church defended,

And thyself to death commended,

Willing thus for Christ to die.

T. THOMAS OF CANTERBURY

Champion! who this life disdains!

Victory in the fight you gains,

And the joyful palm obtainest;

Evidence of which the plainest

All thy wonders rare afford.

To the blind their sight you givest,

And the lame man's powers revivest;

You paralysis relievest,

And the old foe backward drivest,

And transgressions' filthy horde.

Gem of priesthood, princely Thomas!

By thy prayer effectual from us

Take our lusts, our flesh subdue;

That, in Christ, the true Vine, rooted,

We may gain, thus constituted,

Life joys both divine and true! Amen.

T. THOMAS OF CANTERBURY

NOW let our holy Mother Church bemoan

What was aforetime by Great Britain done;

'Twas a deed detestable:

By pious feelings France is deeply stirred,

And in all horror from the guilt abhorred

Flee heaven and earth and seas as well!

Ah! a crime beyond all telling,

One most hateful and repelling,

Was at England's hands then done:

She prejudged her father, newly

To his home restored, and foully

Murdered him upon his throne.

Thomas, all England's brightest flower,

The glory of the church, before

All others in exalted fame,

At Canterbury's temple door.

The laws of justice to secure,

Both sacrifice and priest became.

T. THOMAS OF CANTERBURY

'Twixt the temple and the altar,

On the threshold, each assaulter

Doth rudely shake, but breaks him not;

Though with their swords in twain they cut

In its midst the temple veil.

Low Elisha's bald head lies,

Zacharias, slaughtered, dies;

Peace, thus betrayed, dissolves away,

And the sweet organ now can play

But the tearful mourners' wail.

Upon Childennas's morrow

Is this Innocent to sorrow

Dragged forth, and blows, and tortures' pain;

Whilst, on the earth outpoured, his brain,

Lo! the sword's point bares.

As that temple's chiefest glory,

Blushes still its pavement gory,

Which is o'ersprinkled with his blood,

As there this holy priest of God

Robes of passion wears.

Rages wrath, with fury fevered,

Just blood is to death delivered;

With a sword his head is shivered

In the presence of the Lord:

T. THOMAS OF CANTERBURY

Consecrating, consecrated,

Immolating, immolated,

He to man a celebrated

Type of virtue doth afford.

Holocaust, with marrow welling,

Known to earth's remotest dwelling,

Sacrifice to God sweet smelling,

This pontiff was selected;

For a crown that may be riven

Two fold robes to him are given

On his primate's throne, in heaven

Restored and re erected.

Jews depreciate our fame, Pagans show derision,

Such as worship idols scoff, that our own religion

Should to break its pledge have dared,

Neither have that father spared,

Over Christians reigning,

Rachel weeps for that son, nor finds consolation.

Who thus in his mother's womb meets assassination;

Over whose untimely end

Holy hearts their tears expend,

Bitterly complaining.

This man is that pontiff bright, 65

Whom on heaven's supremest height

Its supernal maker, God,

T. THOMAS OF CANTERBURY

Established in great glory,

When with swords all gory

England's swordsmen smite him.

Since of death he felt no dread,

But surrendered up his head

To welter in his blood,

When he hence was driven

God to highest heaven

Did at once admit him.

Of his death indeed most precious mighty wonders

testify;

Jesus! may he recommend us unto You eternally!

T. THOMAS OF CANTERBURY

Anew Elisha bitter waters heals

With such new sweetness as new salt reveals;

The pot too, which a herb most deadly fills,

He renders harmless by the fat of meal's

New remedy.

Lo! for the flock another wether dies,

And, for the mother slain, the offspring lies:

To light our darkness a new sun doth rise,

Which the long promised year to all supplies

Of Jubilee.

'"Gainst a new Abel doth Cain's malice fight;

Seir's fierceness 'gainst another Jacob's right;

Another Joseph has his brethren's spite,

Seizing with wicked fraud, put out of sight

In these last days.

Sons 'gainst their fathers to rebel have dared,

Not having e'en their mother's bosom spared:

As Bishop Thomas to his death is snared,

Lo! a new chaos, for all earth prepared,

The eye surveys.

T. THOMAS OF CANTERBURY

But Abel covered with great glory falls;

Haran saves Jacob, when for help he calls;

Joseph bears rule within a monarch's walls;

Our Thomas too is crowned in the bright halls

Of highest heaven.

All Englishmen, their joys renewed, are glad,

And Canterbury, new Bethesda made,

Becomes a pool, the sinful soul to aid,

Whence at all times to all around it laid

Salvation's given.

The river Jordan wider tracts streams o'er;

Another and third Naaman seeks its shore;

Siloam's pool spreads further than before.

Whilst heaven far more profusely than of yore

Doth manna rain.

The sun's rays are with double power outpoured;

A mighty son to Hannah is secured;

Another prophet Herod's ruthless sword

With shamelessness yet more to be abhorred

Hath foully slain.

But, slaughtered thus, a full reward has he;

For to the saint for his great sanctity,

And his pure heart's untiring constancy,

Salvation, life, and light most heavenly,

Is freely given.

T. THOMAS OF CANTERBURY

Henceforth he works unnumbered prodigies;

Lepers are cleansed, the devil's legion flies;

Strength for the lame, and sight for blinded eyes,

Speech for the dumb, for sick folk remedies,

He asks of heaven.

A son of Belial blasphemies he swore,

Burning the saint to harm, atones for;

The loss of sight and death did he incur,

An early death, which stopped for evermore

His wrath's fierce stream.

A man, who in the Lord's saint took delight.

And had his eyes put out by bigot spite.

But soon again recovered perfect sight,

Sang constant praises with rejoicing bright

To God's great name.

Crosses, which were by angel fingers made,

When kindly prayers this pious father prayed,

Through heavenly virtue oft great power displayed;

And grain, that heals the Limbs with palsy dead,

On earth is grown.

An offering of two lamps was made, which same

Are lighted up by a celestial flame:

The broken fragments of a vase proclaim

Who has to some blest shrine by fraudful scheme

Dishonor done.

ST. THOMAS OF CANTERBURY

A lad, who with his foot his mother lamed,

Cut off that foot to show himself ashamed;

Soon, when he had this saint's assistance claimed,

He walked upon two feet, as if ne'er maimed,

A wonder rare!

O seaman, who in mystic ship bear'st sway!

Our joyful praises and this grateful lay

To the great King in kindly prayer to day,

Thomas! commend, and us to Him, we pray,

In potent prayer! Amen.

T. GENEVIEVE

GENEVIEVE a holy mirth

Brings forth upon her holy day;

Then let the chastened heart break forth,

The sacrifice of praise to pay!

Blest was that infant's birth of yore,

As Bishop Germain witness bore.

And what in spirit he foreknew

The issue of events proves true.

Upon the virgin's bosom laid,

To mark her spotless chastity,

A medal, that of bronze was made.

Stamped with a cross suspended he.

Genevieve he then endows

With gifts that heaven sent power can boast,

And consecrates through Christian vows

A temple for the Holy Ghost.

T. GENEVIEVE

For striking at the guileless maid

Her mother's eyes lose all their light

The virgin, for her mother sad,

Restores to them their former sight.

Genevieve, the great souled, wears

Her fleshly frame by fasts away,

And joys, bedewing earth with tears,

In martyrdom from day to day.

'Neath angel guidance she surveys

The heavens above and hell below;

And saves, so fervently she prays.

The people from a barbarous foe.

Long doth she with unearthly power

Some workmen's thirst alleviate;

And at a mother's tears restore

Her only son, struck down by fate.

At the pure maiden's earliest prayer

Trembles and quakes all Satan's race;

While rest and peace demoniacs share,

The sickly hope, the guilty grace.

Some waxen tapers in her hand

With heaven sent flame are made to burn;

Its waters too at her command

Back to a river's bed return.

ST. GENEVIEVE

She by her merits, — living still

When dead, — cools down "the Ardents' " fire,

Who in herself before could quell

The flames within of hot desire.

Disease, death, powers of the air,

And elements, all own her sway;

So Genevieve by force of prayer

Makes Nature's laws her will obey.

In very babes Christ's power alone

Works mighty deeds effectually:

To Christ for such great wonders done

All praise and endless glory be! Amen.

T. AGNES

AS we tell once more the fashion

Of this glorious virgin's passion,

Be we kindled to the fight:

As we touch the sacred flower,

Let us breathe the scents that shower

From its sweetness' full delight!

Beautiful and wise and noble,

Agnes now had to the double

Of five years an added three:

Much the prefect's first born loves her,

But to maiden scorn he moves her.

Not submission to his plea.

Wonderful power of faith,

Wondrous virginity,

Wonderful virtue hath

Virgin hearts' constancy!

ST. AGNES

So did the Son of God

Come of His wondrous will,

And in frail flesh abode;

Which is more wondrous still!

Sick, to bed the lover goeth:

When the cause the prefect knoweth,

Quickly seeks he for a cure:

Much now, vowing more, he proffers,

Short lived offerer, short lived offers!

But his gifts are all too poor.

Her doth the prefect, bare,

To outrage vile expose,

But a thick fringe of hair

Christ round her body throws,

And a robe heaven whitened.

One of the angel race

Beside her takes his place;

The den of lust that night

Becomes the abode of light,

And the lewd are frightened.

Her blind lover, most indignant,

Rushes in, and a malignant

Spirit robs him of life breath.

Weeps his father, all are crying,

Rome bewailed a young man dying

By so terrible a death.

T. AGNES

He is raised by Agnes' pleading;

But the crowd, — blind rage misleading! —

For the maid prepare the stake:

Its bright blaze the guilty burns;

'Gainst the fierce the fierce flame turns

For the Most High's honor's sake.

To the Savior thanks she proffers,

To the lictor her throat offers;

Neither fears she when she suffers,

Conscious of her purity.

Agnes! you, thy crown receiving,

At the saving Lamb's side living,

Comfort to thy parents giving,

Bidd'st them mount to joys on high!

Lest they mourn, as dead and buried.

One, to Spouse divine now married,

In a lamb's shape, Christ the story

Of His own and of thy glory

Set before them, spotless maid!

Suffer not our separation

From that Lamb, our One salvation;

Unto Whom devoted wholly,

You didst noble Constance throughly

Heal of sickness by His aid.

Vessel, glorious and elected!

Flower, with scent by naught affected!

 *T. AGNES*

By the angelic choirs respected!

You are as the type erected

Of a maiden's spotless fame.

Off the palm of victory bearing,

Still thy virgin blossom wearing,

Grant we may, unfit appearing

For a special title, share in,

With the saints, their general name! Amen.

****

END OF VOL. I of 3

Credits:

CHISWICK PRESS 1881

Visit us at your local bookstore on the web at our web site:

http://revelationinsight.tripod.com/

E-Mail: Mystic@Orthodox.com

Visit us at your local bookstore on the web at our web site

FREE BOOK offer for visiting our website: "His Daily Bread"

All works <u>always</u> at least 10% off retail, through our store

The Spurgeon Library

Collected Works   Vol. 1-6

1st segment

The Andrew Murray Library

Collected Works   Volumes 1-5

Women of Faith Series

Volumes 1-4

1st segment

Teresa of Avila	Interior Castle
Collected Works	Julian of Norwich
Dialogues	Catherine of Sienna
Passion of Christ	Anne Catherine Emmerich

Works of the "Catholic Classics" Series

Volumes 1-5

1st segment

Explanation of the Rule of St Augustine	Hugh of St. Victor
Treatise of the Spiritual Life Books 1-3	Bishop Morozzo O.Cist
Imitation of Christ	Thomas a' Kempis

Note: vol. 2-4 are fraternal twins writings

2nd segment

Little Book of Wisdom	Henry Suso

Works of the "Desert Fathers" Series

Volumes 1-4

1st segment

Wisdom of the Desert	James O' Hanney
Desert Fathers Books 1 & 2	Countess Hahn-Hahn
Evigarius Essentials	Evigarius

2nd segment

Life and Selected Works	Ephraim the Syrian

Works for the Master

"Philosopher's Palate" Series

Vol. 1-4

1st segment

Divine Names	Pseudo Dionysius
First Principle	Duns Scotus
Boethius	Consolation of Philosophy
Pesenes	Paschal

The Thomas Aquinas Library

Volumes 1-6

1st segment

The Companion to the Summa	Walter Farrell O.P.

2nd segment

Contra Gentiles	Thomas Aquinas

Works for the Journeyman

"Great Christian Mystical Writings"

Volumes 1-5

1ˢᵗ segment

Ascent of Mount Carmel	St. John of the Cross
Dark Night of the Soul	St. John of the Cross
A Cell of Knowledge	Anonymous
Divine Consolation	Angelina Foligno

2ⁿᵈ segment

A Cloud of Unknowing	Walter Hilton

"The Contemplative" Series

Volumes 1-4

1ˢᵗ segment

Ladder of Perfection	Walter Hilton
Selection of Hugh of St Victor	Hugh of St Victor
Third Spiritual Alphabet	Francisco de Osuna
Golden Treatise of Mental Prayer	Peter of Alcantra

French Enlightenment Series

Volumes 1-3

1ˢᵗ segment

Selections	Francis de Fenelon
Selections	Francis de Sales Book. 1&2

Research Essentials" Series

Volumes 1-4

1ˢᵗ segment

Medieval to Modern English Dictionary	R /I Publishing Staff
Contemplative Life	St. Bruno
Ecclesiastical History	Bede
Church Creeds	Various

Works for the Apprentice

The Initial Series

"Pilgrim's Pantry"

Volumes 1-5

1st segment

The Kneeling Christian	Anonymous
Passion of Christ	Bro Smith SGS
Way of Perfection	Teresa of Avila
Augustine Essentials	Augustine

2nd segment

Ascent of the Pilgrim	Various Authors

"The Monastic Series"

Volumes 1-6

1st & 2nd segments

A Short Overview of Monasticism	Alfred Wishart
Monasticism from Egypt to the 4th Cent	W. Mackean

2nd segment

A Monk's Topical Bible in 4 Books.

All these works may be purchased through us directly or from your local bookstore.

Each series will comprise of 12 volumes each.

Visit us at your local bookstore on the web at our web site

FREE BOOK offer for visiting our website:

"His Daily Bread"

All works <u>always</u> at least 10% off retail, through our store

http://revelationinsight.tripod.com/

E-Books in

Kindle

Sony E-Reader

B n' N's Nook

www.ingramcontent.com/pod-product-compliance
Lightning Source LLC
Chambersburg PA
CBHW030140170426
43199CB00008B/146